The Personal Transformation Playbook

Habit Strategies for Lasting Change

Britney E. Kelley

Table of Contents

1. Introduction 2

2. Understanding Habit Formation: The Science Behind Our Behavior 3

    2.1. The Neurological Framework of Habits 3

    2.2. The Role of Dopamine in Habit Formation 4

    2.3. The Power of Habitual Triggers 5

    2.4. In Conclusion: The Power of Habit 5

3. Mastering Your Mind: Techniques for Re-engineering Thoughts .. 6

    3.1. Understanding Thoughts and Their Impact 6

    3.2. The Interplay Between Thoughts, Emotions, and Behaviors ... 7

    3.3. Thought Stopping Techniques 7

    3.4. Cognitive Reappraisal 8

    3.5. Mindfulness and Meditation 8

    3.6. Growth Mindset 8

4. Identifying and Assessing Your Habits: The Good, The Bad, and The Ugly 10

    4.1. Unearthing Your Habits: A Comprehensive Catalog 10

    4.2. Applying the Habit Assessment Lens: Differentiating Between Good, Bad, and Ugly Habits 11

    4.3. The ABC Model: A Tool for Habit Analysis 11

    4.4. Diving Deeper: Unearthing the Why of Habits 12

    4.5. Creating an Actionable Habit Improvement Strategy 12

5. Breaking Free: Strategies for Dismantling Bad Habits 14

    5.1. Unraveling the Core of Bad Habits 14

    5.2. The Habit Loop: Cue, Routine, Reward 15

    5.3. Mindfulness: The Art of Awareness 15

    5.4. The Power of Substitution: Replacing the Bad with the Good 16

5.5. Building a Supportive Environment 16

5.6. Dealing with Setbacks 16

6. Building Blocks: Crafting Positive Habits for a Better You 18

6.1. Why Positive Habits Matter 18

6.2. The Science of Positive Habit Formation 19

6.3. Crafting Your Personal Positive Habits 19

6.4. Harnessing the Power of Mini Habits 20

6.5. Fostering Habit Sustainability 21

7. The Role of Environment: Making Space for Positive Change 23

7.1. The Environment as a Determining Factor 23

7.2. Harnessing Environmental Cues 24

7.3. Creating a Conducive Environment 24

7.4. Altering Your Environment for Lasting Change 25

7.5. Embracing Awareness and Mindfulness 25

8. From Theory to Practice: Translating Strategy into Everyday
Life 27

8.1. Convincing the Mind: Preparing for Change 27

8.2. From Knowledge to Action: Employing Strategy 28

8.3. Setting Up Habit Triggers: Creating Cues for New Habits 28

8.4. Baby Steps: Gradual Implementation 29

8.5. Reflect, Revise, Respond: Continual Improvement 29

9. Staying on Course: Dealing with Setbacks and Challenges 31

9.1. Understanding Your Obstacles 31

9.2. Building a Resilience Kit 31

9.3. Embracing Setbacks as Learning Opportunities 32

9.4. Agile Goal Setting 32

9.5. Leaning on Your Support Network 33

10. Maintenance Mode: Ensuring Your Habits Stick for the Long
Haul 34

10.1. Habit Reinforcement: An Ongoing Process 34

10.2. The Role of Reward Systems 35

10.3. Stress Management and Resistance 35

10.4. Adapting to Changes in Your Life 35

11. Beyond Habits: Embracing Whole-Person Transformation 37

11.1. Embracing Emotional Intelligence 37

11.2. Investing in Physical Health 38

11.3. Cultivating Healthy Relationships 38

11.4. Fostering A Growth Mindset 39

The only way to make sense out of change is to plunge into it, move with it, and join the dance.

— Alan Watts

Chapter 1. Introduction

Discover a reinvigorated, unstoppable you with "The Personal Transformation Playbook: Habit Strategies for Lasting Change", your ultimate guide to cultivating healthier habits and achieving sustainable self-improvement. This Special Report is bursting with scientifically backed tips, easy-to-follow strategies and real-life case studies that will transform your daily routines into potent catalysts for change. There's never been a better time to take the reins of your life and start working towards the best version of you. Don't settle for the same old, same old – embrace the change you deserve with an ounce of determination, a splash of commitment and our essential Playbook. Ready for a fresh chapter? The key to your personal transformation awaits inside!

Chapter 2. Understanding Habit Formation: The Science Behind Our Behavior

There's a fascinating science underpinning habit formation, which sits at the intersection of psychology, neuroscience, and behavioral science. Having a comprehensive understanding of it can therefore be instrumental in implementing lasting beneficial changes in one's life.

2.1. The Neurological Framework of Habits

A habit is essentially a deeply ingrained pattern of behavior that arises from repetitive actions. At the heart of this repetitive nature is the neurological loop pattern, comprising three major components: the cue, the routine or behavior, and the reward.

The 'cue' triggers a particular routine or behavior; it could be a time of the day, a place, or a prevailing emotional state. The 'routine' or 'behavior' is your response to that cue, a series of actions that you automatically take. Lastly, the 'reward' is the outcome of this behavior - something that your brain likes and that reinforces the habit loop. This three-parter neurological loop, cue-routine-reward, serves as the bedrock of habit formation.

While this might seem simple, it's backed by complex processes within the brain. Our brains are designed to save energy. When we perform an action frequently, our brain starts storing this sequence in the basal ganglia, a part of our brain responsible for habits. This automatic storage of sequences means that the brain has to expend less energy once the action becomes a habit, as it no longer requires conscious thought.

This energy conservation aspect makes habits extraordinarily powerful. They dictate almost half of our daily actions and behaviors. Successfully understanding and leveraging this neurological framework can be your first significant step towards self-improvement.

2.2. The Role of Dopamine in Habit Formation

To better understand habit formation, one must explore the role of dopamine. Dopamine, traditionally dubbed the 'feel-good neurotransmitter', is intricately linked with reward processing and habit formation. Activities that stimulate dopamine release provide a sense of pleasure and satisfaction, which the brain then strives to replicate.

In the context of habit formation, the cue triggers the anticipation of a reward, which in turn releases dopamine. This dopamine release makes the subsequent action pleasurable, reinforcing the cue-routine-reward loop.

This might explain why we gravitate towards harmful habits despite their negative ramifications. Habits like excessive internet consumption, binge eating, or heavy smoking can generate a dopamine 'high', and the brain begins craving the dopamine release these habits facilitate.

Recognizing this dopamine effect is key. It focuses on finding healthy habits that provide the dopamine rush without any adverse implications, such as exercise, meditation, or learning a new skill.

2.3. The Power of Habitual Triggers

No discussion of habit formation can be complete without highlighting the role of triggers. These are the events, states, or conditions that set off the habit loop. Developing an awareness of your habit triggers is paramount in modifying, dissolving, or forming new habits.

Habit triggers come in various forms, from external cues such as time and location, to internal cues such as emotional states, thoughts, and preceding actions. For instance, waking up might trigger the habit of brushing your teeth, while an emotional state such as stress might trigger the habit of overeating or smoking.

Identifying these triggers can serve as a powerful tool. By recognizing what drives your habits, you can create a more conducive environment for change. If a certain location triggers an unhealthy habit, modify that environment. If a particular emotional state is a trigger, learn techniques to manage your emotions more effectively.

2.4. In Conclusion: The Power of Habit

To sum it up, habits are powerful drivers of human behavior, designed to conserve the brain's energy. They are neurologically ingrained, and breaking or reforming them involves understanding the complex interplay involving dopamine, the habit loop, and habitual triggers. By comprehending these scientific underpinnings, you can create a strategic, informed plan for lasting self-improvement - the first step being the identification of your existing habits, which brings us to the next chapter of our transformation playbook.

Chapter 3. Mastering Your Mind: Techniques for Re-engineering Thoughts

A large part of personal transformation is harnessing the power of your own thoughts. Every thought we have can set a chain of actions into motion, so mastering the techniques to re-engineer thoughts can be a powerful stepping stone towards meaningful change. This chapter will discuss various approaches to do so; some of them involve mindset shifts, while others require the application of scientifically-backed mental strategies.

3.1. Understanding Thoughts and Their Impact

Life, as we experience it, is greatly influenced by our thoughts. Our perceptions, interpretations, and reactions to the world around us are all shaped by our thoughts. An understanding of the nature of thoughts and how they work in shaping our lives and habits is therefore fundamental to mental mastery.

Thoughts can be spontaneous, or they can occur in reaction to stimuli. Regardless of their origin, the quality of our thoughts affects our emotional state, mental health, and overall well-being. Negative thoughts can lead us into a downward spiral, ultimately culminating in poor self-esteem, depression, or anxiety. Positive thoughts, on the other hand, can uplift us and set the bedrock for joy, confidence, and success.

3.2. The Interplay Between Thoughts, Emotions, and Behaviors

Substantial research shows a strong correlation between thoughts, emotions and behaviors. Understanding this interconnectedness is essential in mastering one's mind. We can think of this interplay as a triangle where each component impacts and is impacted by the others.

This is explained succinctly by Cognitive Behavioral Therapy (CBT), which asserts that people often make interpretations (thoughts) about situations they are in, and these thoughts can influence their emotional states. Consequently, these emotions can drive their behaviors, establishing a cyclical pattern of thought-emotion-behavior.

3.3. Thought Stopping Techniques

Thought stopping is a cognitive intervention technique that helps manage and deal with unwanted or disturbing thoughts. The method follows three basic steps:

1. Identify your disturbing thought.

2. Use a habit interruption tool such as a loud noise or a firm "stop!" command in your mind.

3. Replace the disturbing or negative thought with a positive one.

Over time, this practice will enable you to control the flow of negative thoughts and channel your focus towards more positive and constructive thinking.

3.4. Cognitive Reappraisal

Cognitive reappraisal is a form of cognitive coping strategy that involves changing the way we interpret an emotional stimulus or situation. We consciously try to reduce the emotional impact of a certain stimulus by reevaluating it from a different, more neutral or positive perspective.

For example, if you are feeling anxious about a presentation, you could reappraise the situation by thinking — "This is an opportunity for me to share my knowledge and connect with the team" instead of "I'm going to mess up and everyone is going to judge me."

3.5. Mindfulness and Meditation

Mindfulness is the practice of being present and engaged in the current moment. This technique facilitates an awareness of the thoughts that pass through our minds, without judgment or reaction. Mindfulness meditation can significantly improve mental clarity, focus, and openness, consequently enabling healthier thought patterns and habits.

Moreover, numerous scientific studies vouch for the effectiveness of mindfulness in combating stress, improving mental health, and promoting overall well-being.

3.6. Growth Mindset

Endorsed by psychologist Carol Dweck, the concept of 'Growth Mindset' is a powerful way to re-engineer thoughts. The idea is to adopt a mindset that views the brain's abilities as malleable rather than fixed. By doing so, failures are viewed as opportunities for growth and learning, and not as the end of the road.

Adopting a growth mindset can drastically change your

interpretation of experiences and pave the way for meaningful self-improvement.

In conclusion, personal transformation is inextricably linked to our thoughts. The power to effect change lies in our ability to approach our thought processes consciously, understanding their implications and steering them towards positivity, resilience, and open-mindedness. By mastering skills like thought stopping, cognitive reappraisal, mindfulness, and fostering a growth mindset, we can significantly enhance our mental well-being and catalyze meaningful personal growth.

Chapter 4. Identifying and Assessing Your Habits: The Good, The Bad, and The Ugly

The journey to personal transformation begins by taking a thorough, introspective look into our daily habits: what they are, why they exist, and how they influence our lives. The actions that constitute our day-to-day routines may appear simple, but they bear a lot of weight that can make or break our progress towards personal growth.

4.1. Unearthing Your Habits: A Comprehensive Catalog

To kick-start our journey, it is crucial to consciously think of our habits - to acknowledge them, to pen them down, to create a comprehensive inventory of them. This step can be challenging because habits are typically automatic behaviors. We often carry them out without giving them much thought, often not even realizing we are doing so.

To facilitate this process, you can begin by reflecting upon your daily routine. What are the first actions you undertake when you wake up? What do you typically do on your way to work, and during your lunch break? What is your after-work routine? How do you wind down at the end of the day? These moments probably consist of habits you've cultivated over the years.

Take a week to observe yourself consciously, noting down your actions, reactions, and go-to behaviors at different times and scenarios throughout your day. This activity will help you produce a robust habit catalog, filled with actions large and small that influence your life in more ways than one. These could range from the mundane - making your bed or brushing your teeth - to personalized - perhaps you have a habit of procrastinating on tasks by scrolling social media, or a propensity to take on an extra workload.

4.2. Applying the Habit Assessment Lens: Differentiating Between Good, Bad, and Ugly Habits

With your habit catalog at the ready, the next step is to assess these habits discerningly. Here, the analogy of good, bad, and ugly comes into play.

Good habits are productive behaviors that contribute to personal growth and well-being. They align with your values and help move you closer to your goals. In your catalog, these could be habits such as waking up early, eating a healthy breakfast, or reading a few pages of a book every night.

Bad habits, on the other hand, are those that stunt growth or cause you harm in some way. These could range from consuming junk food regularly, procrastinating on tasks, or spending excessive time on social media.

The ugly habits are the immensely harmful ones. These habits pose a severe threat to your physical, emotional, or mental well-being. This could include smoking, overconsumption of alcohol, perpetuating toxic relationships, or constantly engaging in negative self-talk.

4.3. The ABC Model: A Tool for Habit Analysis

One of the ways you can assess your habits further is by using the

ABC model, a framework borrowed from psychology that stands for Antecedents, Behavior, and Consequences. The "Antecedents" are triggers or situations that often precede the habit. The "Behavior" is the habit itself. Finally, "Consequences" are the immediate outcomes that occur as a result of your behavior. This model can help you understand the triggers and outcomes surrounding each habit, ultimately aiding in their further dissection.

4.4. Diving Deeper: Unearthing the Why of Habits

Harboring a deep understanding of our habits requires exploring beyond just what they are - it requires delving into why they are. Our habits often reveal something about our deep-seated needs, beliefs, fears, and desires. Understanding the underlying motivations that drive your habits can provide you with powerful insights to leverage during the change process.

4.5. Creating an Actionable Habit Improvement Strategy

Having meticulously identified and assessed your habits, you are now equipped with a deep understanding of your daily routines. You are aware of the good, bad, and ugly, and understand the why behind them. Armed with these insights, you are now ready to formulate a personalized, effective habit improvement strategy. This strategy should prioritize tackling the ugly habits first, while enhancing the good and replacing the bad.

Remember, Rome was not built in a day, and your habits will not change overnight either. Lafley & Martin's 'Playing to Win' strategy elucidates that winning is not about embracing one-and-done changes, but about making consistent choices towards victory.

So begin by drawing up a simple, realistic plan, that's challenging yet achievable. It could be replacing one unhealthy snack with a fruit each day, or dedicating just ten minutes towards a desired skill. Be flexible, expect setbacks, but remember to persist. Every small step will contribute to a huge leap in your personal transformation.

The journey of a thousand miles starts with a single step, and identifying and assessing your habits is that critical first step towards your personal transformation. So, dive deep into your routines, be honest with yourself, embrace the journey, and watch as you unfold the best version of you – one habit at a time. Your journey towards lasting change and personal improvement has only just begun.

Chapter 5. Breaking Free: Strategies for Dismantling Bad Habits

Indeed, in our journey of personal transformation, it is crucial to first address the chain that pulls us back: our harmful habits. These behaviors, concealed in our day-to-day life, often function as silent saboteurs, hindering our progress towards the beneficial change we aspire to achieve. Here, we investigate the necessary strategies aimed at disarming these detrimental habits effectively, making room for the creation and consolidation of impactful positive habits.

5.1. Unraveling the Core of Bad Habits

To confront our bad habits effectively, we must first understand their roots. These destructive patterns mostly stem from our attempt to resolve distress or discomfort with a quick, momentarily satisfying solution. The downside? This temporary relief often has long-term repercussions. Recognizing this crucial link between discomfort and indulging in a harmful behavior represents the first step towards overthrowing these habits.

For instance, consider a case where you tend to overeat when overwhelmed by stress. Identifying this link allows a constructive confrontation of the stress, rather than resorting to unhealthy coping mechanisms.

5.2. The Habit Loop: Cue, Routine, Reward

Revisiting the fundamental structure of a habit - the habit loop - offers key insights into the dismantling process. Comprising 'Cue', 'Routine', and 'Reward', the habit loop synthesizes how habits work. The 'Cue' initiates the 'Routine', which is the habit itself, and is followed by the 'Reward', the pleasure or relief that reinforces this cycle.

Disrupting this loop is crucial to breaking free from bad habits. For example, if you routinely check social media whenever you feel bored (Cue), then addressing that boredom with a healthier activity could eliminate the reliance on social media (Routine) while still providing a rewarding experience.

5.3. Mindfulness: The Art of Awareness

Mindfulness, defined as the practice of intentional awareness of the present moment, serves as a powerful tool to break bad habits. Highlighting our automatic reactions and patterns, mindfulness allows us to respond thoughtfully rather than react impulsively, offering an opportunity to choose healthier alternatives.

By deliberately recognizing when and why we engage in a bad habit, we can create a pause in the habit loop, paving the way for mindful intervention and eventually habit transformation.

5.4. The Power of Substitution: Replacing the Bad with the Good

One of the most effective strategies for breaking bad habits involves replacing them with healthier ones. While completely eliminating a routine can leave a void, substituting it with a beneficial habit can fill this gap and provide a more fulfilling reward.

Instead of annihilating a habit completely, repurpose the ingrained energy of the habit loop towards a more supportive behavior. For instance, if a daily coffee intake leads to caffeine dependence, try substitifying coffee with herbal tea. The act of drinking remains, but the substance changes, thereby striking a balance between habit change and habit maintenance.

5.5. Building a Supportive Environment

The desired internal change is often directly proportional to the environment we surround ourselves with. An environment conducive to old, destructive habits limits our capacity to foster new behaviors. By consciously crafting an environment that supports and eases the transition into healthier habits, the journey of personal change becomes smoother and more achievable.

This undertaking might look like decluttering your space to encourage tidiness or storing junk food beyond easy reach to support healthier eating habits.

5.6. Dealing with Setbacks

Recognizing that setbacks are part of the process is essential for sustained habit transformation. Instances of reverting to old habits should not deter our progress. Instead, treating setbacks as learning experiences allows us to fine-tune our strategies, catalyzing our growth further.

When faced with a setback, conducting a self-reflection exercise to identify weaknesses in our strategy can be especially useful. Adopting an empathetic approach towards self, allows us to weather the storm of setbacks, and steadily sail towards the shores of sustainable transformation.

In conclusion, as we navigate the flux of life, understanding and dismantling our detrimental habits are seminal towards our personal growth. This chapter captured a multitude of strategies such as decoding the habit loop, adopting mindfulness, habit substitution, environment redesign, and resilient approach towards setbacks. Implementing these elements strategically offers us a promising vista into the compelling journey of personal transformation, marking the exit from the realm of harmful habits and our entry into a domain of powerful, positive patterns that align with our aspirations.

Chapter 6. Building Blocks: Crafting Positive Habits for a Better You

Starting on the path of constructing potent and life-changing habits demands an understanding of why some habits positively contribute to our well-being, while others do the exact opposite. Before we delve into the thorough process of constructing beneficial habits for an improved self, it's critical to comprehend the power of these unseen forces that govern our lives.

6.1. Why Positive Habits Matter

To paint a broader picture, let's highlight why positive habits are so fundamental. A habit, essentially, is a regularly repeated behavior pattern that requires minimal conscious thought. The 'positive' in positive habits denotes that these ceaseless behavioral patterns contribute to our psychological, physical, or emotional well-being and growth.

Modern psychological research espouses the theory that our habits account for around 40% of our actions at any given day. Imagine the multiplying impact of positive habits on our lives if they constitute such a substantial chunk of our daily behavior. Over time, positive habits can significantly influence personal development, boost confidence, improve health and fitness, enrich relationships, enhance productivity, and lead to success in multiple facets of life.

6.2. The Science of Positive Habit Formation

The process of forming a habit involves a neurological pattern called a "habit loop," which comprises three elements: a cue, a routine, and a reward. In his well-known book, "The Power of Habit," Charles Duhigg offers extensive insight into these elements collectively responsible for engraining habits into our lives. The formation of a positive habit usually follows the same framework.

1. **Cue:** The cue, also known as a trigger, stimulates the brain to perform the habit. It could be a time of day, location, emotional state, or preceding action. Understanding cues is crucial in the habit-forming process.

2. **Routine:** This refers to the behavior executed in response to the cue. In positive habit formation, this is the beneficial action we want to make habitual, such as exercising, eating healthily, or practicing gratitude.

3. **Reward:** This component provides positive reinforcement for performing the routine, incentivizing the habit loop's continuation. It conditions the brain to anticipate this gratification each time the cue occurs.

Repeated enactment of this loop eventually leads to its automation, forming a 'positive habit.' However, habit formation is far from a mere scientific process, but rather an art that requires self-understanding, creativity, and patience.

6.3. Crafting Your Personal Positive Habits

There are numerous habits leading to personal betterment, but the key to crafting them lies in knowing what's most beneficial for YOU.

Indeed, each individual's positive habits are inherently personal and may vary according to their goals, lifestyle, and values. One might find mental peace in daily meditation, while another might thrive with regular physical exercise, and yet another with self-reflective journaling.

To figure out which positive habits you want to cultivate, one useful approach involves answering some introspective questions to better understand yourself and your aspirations. Reflect on what you truly desire: Is it physical health? Mental stability? Career growth? Relationship improvement? Next, consider the actions that could lead to these outcomes. What small, doable behaviors, when repeated consistently, can help you to achieve this desired state?

After identifying these habits, shift your focus to how you can insert them into your existing daily routine. This is where Duhigg's habit loop comes into play. Discern the cues and rewards that can be associated with your identified routine to solidify the habit. Be experimental and adaptable during these steps. It's important to note that results aren't instantaneous, but with patience and staunch perseverance, the benefits will follow.

6.4. Harnessing the Power of Mini Habits

One of the greatest hindrances to implementing positive habits is the ambitious nature of our goals, which often leads to overwhelming ourselves. A helpful alternative to setting intimidating goals is to break them down into "mini habits." Devised by Stephen Guise, this strategy involves creating extremely small and easily achievable goals for habit building.

For example, if you wish to adopt a habit of reading, start by reading just one page a day. This task is so simple that there's almost no resistance. After settling into the routine, gradually increase the goal.

Apart from being less overwhelming, mini habits capitalize on the principle of 'compounding effect' - the accumulation of repeated, small habits over time leads to remarkable results. Guise's concept simplifies the habit formation journey and makes it attainable, fostering self-belief and continuity.

6.5. Fostering Habit Sustainability

Creating a positive habit is only half the battle - the real success lies in sustaining it. Understandably, you will face challenges, but it's crucial not to let setbacks hinder your progress. Remember, it's the long-term trend that matters more than daily perfection.

A crucial technique to ensure sustainability is 'habit stacking.' It involves integrating the new habit with a pre-existing one. Resultantly, the established habit acts as a strong cue for the new one, reinforcing adherence.

Additionally, self-monitoring assists in keeping track of your progress. Be it using a habit tracking app, a journal, or a simple checking system, recording consistency fosters accountability and motivation.

Above all, nurturing a positive mindset plays a paramount role in habit sustainability. Maintain an optimistic outlook, appreciate your small wins, and remember that setbacks are not failures but integral constituents of the journey.

In conclusion, crafting positive habits for a better you involves building an intricate balance between scientific understanding and personalized strategies. It's not just about adopting universally acclaimed habits; it's constructing habits that resonate with your personal goals and values, combining the principles of habit formation, mini habits, and habit sustainability. With patience, consistency, and self-belief, the empowering transformation that positive habits bring about awaits you! Embrace this journey as you sculpt a better version of yourself, one habit at a time.

Chapter 7. The Role of Environment: Making Space for Positive Change

One cannot underestimate the power and profound influence of the environment on our habits. While intrinsic motivation and personal willpower contribute significantly to habit formation and personal transformation, the environment, in its broadest sense, serves as a steadfast foundation upon which personal growth and development can occur.

7.1. The Environment as a Determining Factor

The environment plays a pivotal role in shaping our habits and behavior. It provides the context and the cues that trigger habitual actions, nudging us towards specific responses. Environmental cues can often bypass our conscious thinking, leading us to behave in ways that align with the environmental context – whether it's your body's innate response to turn off the alarm clock in the morning or automatically reach for a snack when you're watching TV in the evening.

Our surroundings have a considerable unconscious control over our daily actions. Various studies reveal that people who live in cluttered spaces are more likely to feel stressed and less productive. This is because our environment reflects and affects our internal state. A cluttered space reflects a cluttered mind and, conversely, an organized, clean environment signals control and order, encouraging positive habits and behaviors.

7.2. Harnessing Environmental Cues

Understanding how environmental cues can inform our behavior gives us a powerful tool to implement positive change in our lives. By consciously shaping our environment, we can design an external world that encourages and reinforces our desired habits.

Consider the following example: If you aim to incorporate healthier eating habits, keeping fresh fruits and vegetables in plain sight increases the likelihood that you'll reach for those when you're hungry, rather than opting for junk food stashed away in the cupboard. The arrangement of objects in your environment, such as readily accessible exercise equipment or books placed on your bedside table, can serve as constant reminders and cues for healthy habits.

7.3. Creating a Conducive Environment

We should strive to construct an environment where good habits are not only possible but are also the most convenient choice. This might involve removing temptations from our immediate surroundings to reduce the chances of falling back into old habits. For example, if you wish to reduce your screen time, keeping your electronic devices out of your bedroom eliminates the temptation to check social media first thing in the morning and last thing at night. Remember, out of sight is often out of mind.

Creating an environment conducive to positive change also involves fostering a supportive social environment. Surrounding yourself with positive influences, people who share your goals, aspirations, and values, can fortify your resolve and determination, driving you toward successful personal transformation.

7.4. Altering Your Environment for Lasting Change

Achieving lasting change requires more than establishing new habits; you need to sustain these habits. Altering your environment is a highly efficient tool to ensure that newly formed routines stick. Changing the shape and structure of our daily environment can help automatic behaviors become cemented into place. For instance, if your objective is to exercise regularly, joining a local gym or creating a mini workout space at home can facilitate and support this positive habit.

Additionally, consider travel and change of scenery as a form of environment shaping. Immersing yourself in new surroundings can provide fresh perspectives and stimulate personal growth. Furthermore, traveling can create an environment that disrupts established patterns, giving you the chance to break free from entrenched routines and develop new habits.

7.5. Embracing Awareness and Mindfulness

Finally, the cultivation of awareness and mindfulness plays a crucial role in successfully modifying your environment. Being aware of the influence your surroundings have on your behavior enables you to anticipate environmental challenges and remain vigilant in your path towards transformation.

In conclusion, the role of the environment in habit formation is monumental. It acts as a silent trigger, constantly nudging us toward specific actions and reactions. By consciously shaping our environment to foster positive habits, we can embark on a journey of personal transformation that is sustainable and deeply rooted in our day-to-day life. A personalized, supportive environment designed with purpose and intentionality becomes an ally in our pursuit of personal growth and self-fulfillment.

Chapter 8. From Theory to Practice: Translating Strategy into Everyday Life

The chapter begins with the understanding that the coalescence of theory and practice is pivotal for the true embodiment of personal transformation. The seamless melding of what we 'know' and what we 'do' unlocks the doors to lasting change and habit reformulation. This sacred union of knowledge and action illuminates the pathway to self-improvement, providing us with the guiding compass we need in our transformational journey. Having set this context, we delve now into the ways of embodying theoretical learning and converting it into practical application.

8.1. Convincing the Mind: Preparing for Change

Deeply ingrained habits and thought patterns can prove resistant to change because our minds rely on well-established neural pathways. It's akin to sitting comfortably on a plush, well-worn couch - it's familiar and safe. However, stepping out of this comfort zone is the first step towards transformation. A crucial part of making this shift involves convincing your mind that it is ready for and capable of change, a process that necessitates fostering positivity and openness.

Strategies like mindfulness practice, meditation, and reinforcement of self-belief can stimulate mental readiness. Dedicate a few minutes every day to reflect upon yourself, explore your feelings, and visualize the improved version of you that will emerge after implementing your well-designed strategies. Remember, convincing your mind for change is no less significant than the change itself.

8.2. From Knowledge to Action: Employing Strategy

Taking the leap from absorbing knowledge to applying it in your daily routine can seem daunting. Familiarizing yourself with the cognitive processes and the psychological underpinnings of habit formation is insightful. But, the real change materializes when theories are translated into concrete actions. This transition is facilitated by either reinventing existing routines or creating new ones.

The effectiveness of a habit change strategy hinges on its practical adaptability. Hence, it is indispensable that you tailor strategies to your lifestyle and preferences to ensure that they are viable yet challenging. Perceive this process not as an uphill struggle, but as an exciting exploration to map out the nexus between theory and practice.

8.3. Setting Up Habit Triggers: Creating Cues for New Habits

After convincing your mind and employing strategies, the next step is to identify habit triggers or cues. These signals in your environment are crucial in sparking the behavior. Research shows that consistent cues are potent enablers in fostering new habits.

For instance, if you're trying to instill a daily reading habit, a trigger could be placing a book on your nightstand every night. Thus, every time you retire for the night, the sight of the book will prompt you to read. Instituting effective habit triggers is an instrumental aspect of habit formation that will aid you in converting strategies into action.

8.4. Baby Steps: Gradual Implementation

Change, especially at the individual level, doesn't happen overnight. It's a gradual process. Start with feasible challenges, gradually upping the ante as your comfort with the new habit increases. This prevents overwhelming your system and gives you a chance to adjust at every stage.

Rewarding yourself appropriately at each milestone allows for positive reinforcement, which facilitates continuation and prevents relapse. For instance, if you're trying to reduce screen time, initially, just reducing an hour could be rewarding in itself. Over time, you can increase the number of hours according to your comfort level.

8.5. Reflect, Revise, Respond: Continual Improvement

The transformational journey is not a one-track road. There may be times when strategies need re-evaluation and modifications. Adopt a seeker's attitude and continually reflect upon your progress. Make revisions as needed and respond to these assessments with refined strategies.

For example, if you find your meditation regime challenging to keep up with, consider revising your strategy – maybe shorten the duration or change the time you practice. Stay responsive to feedback from your journey, and don't be afraid to adapt your approach as you evolve.

We conclude the chapter with a reminder that the path to self-improvement is as unique as an individual's fingerprint, meaning there's no 'one-size-fits-all' solution. Developing a personalized approach that synergizes theoretical understanding with everyday practices is crucial. Keep in mind, it takes resilience, determination, patience, and self-belief to translate strategy into life. Embrace the journey, cherish the transformative process, and celebrate the growth and changes that blossom each day. Change is never linear, but the destination of personal transformation is worth every effort.

Chapter 9. Staying on Course: Dealing with Setbacks and Challenges

Preparing yourself for the inevitable ups and downs that accompany any journey of self-improvement is a pivotal step towards achieving lasting change. As much as we'd like to imagine a seamless path from current to desired self, the reality is often fraught with challenges and setbacks. These stumbling blocks are a natural part of the transformative process, and while they may seem overwhelming in the moment, they provide valuable lessons that contribute to your overall growth.

9.1. Understanding Your Obstacles

The first step to staying on course is understanding and identifying the common obstacles that come your way. These challenges can come in many forms - external factors such as work and family commitments, physical conditions like illness or fatigue, and internal influences such as self-doubt or lack of motivation.

Quit seeing these obstacles as roadblocks halting your journey entirely, but tread them as speed bumps that merely slow you down temporarily. Remember, the essence of transformation isn't about a perfectly linear journey, but progress despite life's unavoidable complications.

9.2. Building a Resilience Kit

Developing a resilience kit is an essential step in preparing yourself for setbacks. This could include a variety of strategies handpicked for their effectiveness in boosting your resolve and fortitude.

A personal mantra, ideally a phrase or sentence that brings you comfort or inspiration, can serve you well when faced with adversity. Mindfulness techniques such as meditation or focused breathing exercises can also empower you in managing your emotions and maintaining relatively healthy stress levels.

Embrace an attitude of self-compassion – be kind to yourself and appreciate that imperfections and slip-ups are part of the human experience.

9.3. Embracing Setbacks as Learning Opportunities

We push forward by learning from our failures, not by berating ourselves for them. Failures and setbacks could be reframed as stepping stones that form the roadmap to success. By focusing less on setbacks being setbacks and more on the lessons they can provide, you can fuel your motivation to push forward.

Analyze your setbacks, find the triggers, understand your responses, and uncover what went wrong. This analysis will provide insights into behavioral patterns and help you fine-tune your response for the future.

9.4. Agile Goal Setting

An integral part of your journey should be revisiting your goals regularly to ensure they are still relevant and realistic. This agility in goal setting gives you the flexibility to adapt your course as you learn more about yourself, your strengths, and your weaknesses.

Avoid holding yourself rigidly to the same targets if circumstances or your understanding of them has changed. Providing yourself with the freedom to evolve your objectives keeps your journey dynamic and responsive to your personal growth.

10.2. The Role of Reward Systems

Rewards play a pivotal role in the habit loop. They trigger the release of pleasure chemicals in the brain such as dopamine, creating a sense of satisfaction. To ensure your newly formed habits stick, it's crucial to establish a meaningful and consistent reward system.

It's a misstep to think of rewards only in terms of material possessions or guilty pleasures. Instead, the most compelling rewards are those linked directly to your habit. Perhaps it's the rush of endorphins from a good workout, the satisfaction from a completed project, or the peace from a meditation session. These intrinsic rewards are more sustainable and satisfying in the long run.

10.3. Stress Management and Resistance

Every change, regardless of its positive impact, induces a level of stress. Resisting former habits, overcoming temptiness or even managing the expectations of success can escalate stress levels.

To handle this, prioritize stress management techniques in your daily routine. Physical methods such as exercise, proper sleep and diet play an integral role. Mental techniques like mindfulness, mediation, and cognitive reframing—viewing stressors in a positive or neutral light—are equally important. Moreover, learning to accept imperfections and lapses and using them as learning opportunities can significantly diminish stress-related resistance.

10.4. Adapting to Changes in Your Life

Life is unpredictable—changes, both internal and external, are inevitable. New jobs, relationships, locations, or even personal growth can alter your habits significantly.

To maintain your progress amidst shifting circumstances, stay flexible and adaptive. Craft your habits such that they can mold to fit different settings and routines. Resilience-building exercises, such as cognitive flexibility drills, improvisation tasks, and change-embracing mindfulness techniques, can guide you towards maintaining your habitual formation process amidst transformations.

In conclusion, maintaining habits for the long haul is an intricate balance of continuous reinforcement, rewarding appropriately, managing resistance, and adapting to life's constant changes. As you continue this journey of personal transformation, hold onto the fact that every effort, no matter how small, contributes meaningfully towards the unstoppable you. Remember that personal transformation is not a sprint, but a marathon. With patience, perseverance, and the strategies outlined herein, you're well on your way to lasting change.

Chapter 11. Beyond Habits: Embracing Whole-Person Transformation

Step by step, we've journeyed through an elaborate exploration of human behavior, specifically concerning habit formation, the processes involved, and effective strategies to form positive habits and dismantle negatives ones. As we delve into our final segment, it's crucial to spread our lens beyond merely habit manipulation and veer towards a broader aspect of self-improvement that encompasses an all-round, whole-person transformation. This whole-person transformation is not isolated to reshuffling our habits but encapsulates metamorphoses in our behavior, thought processes, emotional intelligence, social relationships, and even physical aspects.

11.1. Embracing Emotional Intelligence

Emotional intelligence is a critical pillar of whole-person transformation. It gives us a richer understanding of ourselves, helping us interact more effectively with the world around us. Emotional intelligence is made up of five components: Self-awareness, self-regulation, motivation, empathy, and social skills. Each element plays a significant role in our overall well-being.

- **Self-awareness** involves being in tune with our emotions, strengths, and weaknesses and being conscious of the impact our actions have on others.

- **Self-regulation**, the second component, relates to our ability to control or redirect disruptive impulses and moods. Exercising self-regulation keeps us grounded, clear-headed, and focused in a dynamic world.

- Next comes **Motivation**, the driving force that propels us to achieve our goals despite facing obstacles, discouragement, or failure. It's the intrinsic motivation, the deep-seated desire for success or achievement that drives individuals to make radical changes.

- **Empathy**, the ability to understand and share the feelings of others, is a quality that fosters deeper, more meaningful relationships.

- Lastly, **Social skills** involve the proficiency to manage relationships, induce desirable responses in others, and build a network of supportive, encouraging individuals.

As we strive for whole-person transformation, it's essential to nurture and enhance these competencies.

11.2. Investing in Physical Health

While we've primarily focused on mental and emotional change, physical health is also an indispensable component of whole-person transformation. Diet, regular exercise, adequate sleep, regular medical check-ups, and avoiding harmful substances like excessive alcohol and tobacco, are all parts of a healthy physical regimen. Inculcating good diets (rich in fruits, vegetables, and lean proteins), as well as regular physical activity, can imbue your life with newfound energy and vigor, making you feel more organized, confident, and ready to tackle your goals.

11.3. Cultivating Healthy Relationships

Our relationships play a crucial role in shaping our wellbeing.

Unhealthy relationships can drain us emotionally, while healthy ones can give us energy, joy, and support. Be intentional about the people you share your life with and foster relationships that align with your values and goals. Learn to communicate effectively, assert your needs, take responsibility for your actions, and, most importantly, listen. Successfully engaging with the world lies in your ability to build and maintain healthy relationships.

11.4. Fostering A Growth Mindset

Stanford psychologist Carol Dweck's work distinguishes between a fixed mindset and a growth mindset. Individuals with a fixed mindset maintain a static view of their talents and intelligence, often avoiding challenges for fear of failure. In contrast, individuals with a growth mindset believe that talents and abilities can be developed through dedication and hard work. Embrace a growth mindset to breed resilience and maintain motivation in the face of obstacles.

Achieving whole-person transformation is a journey, not a destination. It's about adapting, growing, learning, and continuously striving to better oneself each passing day. As we close this playbook, remember that change is a process. It's about the small choices you make each day that compound over time to yield transformative results. There's no shortcut or quick fix, but the journey, as challenging as it may seem, is worth every step. With determination, patience, and practice, you're on the path to becoming an improved version of yourself. Congratulations on the journey so far and all the very best for the road ahead!